HERITAGE

by Stephen Churchett

‖SAMUEL FRENCH‖

samuelfrench.co.uk

THINKING ABOUT PERFORMING A SHOW?

There are thousands of plays and musicals available to perform from Samuel French right now, and applying for a licence is easier and more affordable than you might think

From classic plays to brand new musicals, from monologues to epic dramas, there are shows for everyone.

Plays and musicals are protected by copyright law, so if you want to perform them, the first thing you'll need is a licence. This simple process helps support the playwright by ensuring they get paid for their work and means that you'll have the documents you need to stage the show in public.

Not all our shows are available to perform all the time, so it's important to check and apply for a licence before you start rehearsals or commit to doing the show.

LEARN MORE & FIND THOUSANDS OF SHOWS

Browse our full range of plays and musicals, and find out more about how to license a show

www.samuelfrench.co.uk/perform

Talk to the friendly experts in our Licensing team for advice on choosing a show and help with licensing

plays@samuelfrench.co.uk   020 7387 9373

Acting Editions

BORN TO PERFORM

Playscripts designed from the ground up to work the way you do in rehearsal, performance and study

---

Larger, clearer text for easier reading

Wider margins for notes

Performance features such as character and props lists, sound and lighting cues, and more

---

+ CHOOSE A SIZE AND STYLE TO SUIT YOU

  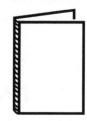

STANDARD EDITION

Our regular paperback book at our regular size

SPIRAL-BOUND EDITION

The same size as the Standard Edition, but with a sturdy, easy-to-fold, easy-to-hold spiral-bound spine

LARGE EDITION

A4 size and spiral bound, with larger text and a blank page for notes opposite every page of text – perfect for technical and directing use

LEARN MORE | **samuelfrench.co.uk/actingeditions**

MUSIC USE NOTE

Licensees are solely responsible for obtaining formal written permission from copyright owners to use copyrighted music in the performance of this play and are strongly cautioned to do so. If no such permission is obtained by the licensee, then the licensee must use only original music that the licensee owns and controls. Licensees are solely responsible and liable for all music clearances and shall indemnify the copyright owners of the play(s) and their licensing agent, Samuel French, against any costs, expenses, losses and liabilities arising from the use of music by licensees. Please contact the appropriate music licensing authority in your territory for the rights to any incidental music.

USE OF COPYRIGHT MUSIC

A licence issued by Samuel French Ltd to perform this play does not include permission to use the incidental music specified in this copy.

Where the place of performance is already licensed by the PERFORMING RIGHT SOCIETY (PRS) a return of the music used must be made to them. If the place of performance is not so licensed then application should be made to the PRS, 2 Pancras Square, London, N1C 4AG.

A separate and additional licence from PHONOGRAPHIC PERFORMANCE LTD, 1 Upper James Street, London W1F 9DE (www.ppluk.com) is needed whenever commercial recordings are used.

IMPORTANT BILLING AND CREDIT REQUIREMENTS

If you have obtained performance rights to this title, please refer to your licensing agreement for important billing and credit requirements.

Other plays by STEPHEN CHURCHETT
licensed by Samuel French

Tom and Clem

FIND PERFECT PLAYS TO PERFORM AT
www.samuelfrench.co.uk/perform

ABOUT THE AUTHOR

Stephen adapted Raymond Briggs' book *Ethel & Ernest* for ACT Productions and the Ambassador Theatre Group. The production opened at Nottingham Playhouse, directed by Giles Croft. Stephen's first play, *Tom & Clem*, opened at the Yvonne Arnaud Theatre in Guildford before transferring to the Aldwych Theatre. It was produced by Michael Codron, directed by Richard Wilson, and starred Michael Gambon and Alec McCowen. *Tom & Clem* was nominated for the Laurence Olivier Awards in the category of Best New Play. *Heritage* opened at Hampstead Theatre before a short tour and starred George Cole, Gwen Taylor and Tim Pigott-Smith.

Heritage had its first performance at Hampstead Theatre (Artistic Director, Jenny Topper), by arrangement with Michael Codron, on 2 December 1997, and was subsequently presented by Michael Codron and Lee Dean. The cast was as follows:

HARRY	George Cole
GEORGE	Tim Pigott-Smith
RUPE	Gideon Turner
MAY	Gwen Taylor
GINNY	Judy Flynn
Director	Mark Rayment
Designer	Johan Engels
Lighting Designer	Howard Harrison
Sound Designer	John A. Leonard

CHARACTERS

HARRY

GEORGE

RUPE

MAY

GINNY

For Sue and Toby

ACT ONE

Scene One

*Spring. Afternoon. Part of a formally informal garden.
An asphalt path runs from one side of the stage to the
other. On the grass a wooden park bench faces the path.
A litter bin is near by. The trunk of an old tree is a short
distance from the bench which is overhung by a bough.
Behind the bench the grass slopes gently and irregularly
upwards, dotted with shrubs and bushes, beyond which
can be glimpsed the red brick of a grand late seventeenth-
early eighteenth-century building. A football rolls into
view. From another direction,* HARRY *enters. He is in
his mid-seventies, wearing the blue sergeant's uniform
of an in-pensioner at the Royal Hospital, Chelsea. He
is carrying a newspaper. He calls in the direction from
which the ball came.*

HARRY There is a notice. (*He kicks the ball back, starts to
turn away, then turns back, putting up two fingers.*) Yes,
you too, son.

*He moves to the tree, places both hands on the trunk,
and stands looking up into the branches.* GEORGE *enters.
He's in his early fifties, wearing a suit and carrying a
small closed umbrella.*

GEORGE You'll get stuck. It'll be the fire brigade.

HARRY Hello, boy. What day is it?

GEORGE Tuesday.

HARRY Thought it was. You should have said.

GEORGE I can drop in, can't I?

HARRY Of course, boy. Nice to see you.

They embrace.

Does it mean you're not coming Friday?

GEORGE Lunch, yes. Pub again?

HARRY See how I feel. If we can get a seat outside.

GEORGE We'll go early.

HARRY You're very spruced up. Suit?

GEORGE Something I had to come up for. Thought I'd drop by.

HARRY Shoes could do with a polish. What's that? Mud?

GEORGE It was still raining this morning. I looked for you in the snooker room. Tuesday.

HARRY Not today. Got a visitor. Rupert's coming.

GEORGE Are you sure?

HARRY I'm not gaga.

GEORGE No. May didn't say, that's all.

HARRY When?

GEORGE I...spoke to her. This morning.

HARRY Oh.

GEORGE That'll be a first, won't it?

HARRY What?

GEORGE Rupe coming to see you alone, without his mother.

HARRY Something to do with college. He's bringing a tape recorder.

GEORGE I'd have thought he'd know your stories backwards by now.

HARRY Who says I'm going to tell my stories?

GEORGE It'll be his "verbal interaction module" or some such thing.

HARRY He wants to know about getting old. Being old.

GEORGE Can't he wait? Find out for himself?

HARRY I don't mind, if it helps the lad. It's for his course.

GEORGE Be nice if he'd come and see you when he doesn't want something, that's all.

HARRY Be fair, boy. How often did you go and see my old man, unless me or your mother took you?

GEORGE I suppose. Didn't I really?

HARRY You said you didn't like the smell. "Old man smell", you used to say.

GEORGE The house. Not him. Did I? God, sorry.

HARRY No need. Just don't think bad of Rupert.

GEORGE I only see him at Christmas, anyway.

HARRY May says she's always asking you over. You never go.

GEORGE Well. What *were* you doing with the tree?

HARRY Just touching. Feeling. It's only a hundred and fifty.

GEORGE Only?

HARRY I'd have put it older.

GEORGE You've seen the papers?

HARRY Is that why you came?

GEORGE I just dropped in, that's all. Coincidence.

HARRY They can't take it any higher. That's it.

GEORGE I'm sorry.

HARRY This is the first to go. These gardens. Underground car park.

GEORGE I saw.

HARRY They'll have their work cut out, with some of them roots.

GEORGE You'll still have the other gardens.

HARRY No trees, though.

GEORGE Nearer for you.

HARRY I don't have trouble walking. Yet. Not like some of them.

GEORGE No.

HARRY We lost Ronnie the week before last.

GEORGE Oh, dear. Sorry. Did I know him?

HARRY Yes, you remember Ronnie. You had a drink with him last year. Founder's Day. Geordie.

GEORGE With big side-whiskers. Yes.

HARRY Ninety-one. Very sudden. He always was a lucky bugger. I wonder how long it'll take?

GEORGE What?

HARRY Before we're all gone. Last admissions this year, no more after that.

GEORGE It'll be years.

HARRY I know it'll be years. The question is, how many?

GEORGE Years, that's all.

HARRY They're going to wait until they can fit us all into North East Wing before they start on the big work.

GEORGE You said.

HARRY We drop off the twig one by one until they can fit us all in there.

GEORGE It might be a nice change for you, different wing.

HARRY There's over twenty different trees in here, different kinds.

GEORGE What's that one, coming into blossom? You can just see it through there.

HARRY Hawthorn.

GEORGE Yes.

HARRY That's why we called your sister "May". Another name for it.

GEORGE I'd forgotten.

HARRY You're getting old.

GEORGE Oh, thanks.

HARRY Used to be a great profusion of hawthorn near the old house when we were there. Your mother loved the May blossom. Used to put it in jars all over the place. Remember that? Remember saving all the jam jars?

GEORGE I think so.

HARRY Couldn't move for them this time of year. On the landing, in the kazi, the scullery, up the shed. Came on leave once and she'd tied some on the front-door knocker.

GEORGE I do remember. I used to help her. "Let's do a nice arrangement." I'd forgotten.

HARRY That's something I can tell Rupert. That you start to remember things from further back.

GEORGE Make sure you don't forget.

HARRY Bit of respect, you. How's business?

GEORGE We haven't opened much lately.

HARRY Been buying?

GEORGE A few sales, house clearances. Local, mostly.

The sound of an approaching helicopter.

HARRY Up for a sale today? Good stuff? Any joy?

GEORGE No.

HARRY How's your mate?

GEORGE He has got a name.

HARRY Yes, I know. All right. Stephen.

The helicopter is now overhead.

GEORGE Stefan.

HARRY What?

They both look up and wait until the noise diminishes.

What?

GEORGE His name's Stefan. Just once, Dad.

HARRY Sorry. Yes. All right.

GEORGE Bloody things. Talk about noisy neighbours. Why can't they go by car or train like anyone else?

HARRY They have to be places ruddy sharpish, the top brass from there. Probably going somewhere hush-hush.

GEORGE Probably going to the golf club.

HARRY You old cynic.

GEORGE That's what I used to say to you.

HARRY You got that off your mother. That's what she used to call *me*.

GEORGE Not without reason.

HARRY A realist, that's what I am. Have to be, with what's going on now. Jake was here last week.

GEORGE He's started now, hasn't he? Yes, May said she'd tell him to find you and say hello.

HARRY *I* saw *him* first. With some of the big-wigs, over by the chapel.

GEORGE Carrying his theodolite at a jaunty angle, no doubt.

HARRY He had someone with him for that.

GEORGE He would, now.

HARRY A theodolite wallah.

GEORGE Yes. *(He laughs longer than one might expect, then suddenly goes to the tree and places both hands on it, looking upwards.)* There *is* something about them.

HARRY They last. And they make sure *we* do. That's why I had your mother buried near a tree. That's why I want to be next to her. Or scattered. Whatever you decide. I'll leave it up to you.

GEORGE Dad.

HARRY Good fertilizer, that's what it comes down to, George. You feed the earth. The roots of the tree feed on the soil. The tree grows. It gives off carbon dioxide. That mixes with oxygen. Someone breathes in, near the tree, they're breathing in some of you. Even if they're miles away they'll still get a tiny bit of you, even just a tiny little bit. See? That's how we last. That's my theory, anyway, and I'm sticking to it.

GEORGE What's brought this on?

HARRY What?

GEORGE You've never talked about this before.

HARRY You don't, do you?

GEORGE You're all right?

HARRY Constitution of the proverbial, that's what the quack said last time.

GEORGE Good.

In the distance a clock chimes the quarter hour.

What time's Rupe due?

HARRY He's a bit late.

A mobile phone rings. GEORGE *looks around to see where it is.* HARRY *produces the phone from his pocket.*

Christmas. From May and Jake. Bang up to date, your old man. Tiny little gizmo.

GEORGE Answer it, then.

HARRY *does.*

HARRY *(to phone)* O three seven four two three six one nine two...speaking...talk of the devil...no matter...got your Uncle George here at the moment...oh, he's fine...see you in a minute then...oh, Rupert, we're outside, it being so nice, in the gardens, so come in the London Gate, the bench opposite the popular tree, remember? ...I know, but that's what you used to call it...yes, don't you remember? ...right-oh. *(He hangs up.)* He's at the station, just walking down. Stuck in a tunnel for twenty minutes. I thought he'd remember about the popular tree. It was the one he could never get right. You remember that?

GEORGE Vaguely.

HARRY Got all the others off pat, even the tricky ones, but he always said "popular". Eight, was he?

GEORGE I don't know.

HARRY Might have been nine.

GEORGE Could have been, yes.

HARRY No. Eight, I reckon.

GEORGE Anyway.

HARRY Well, we can work it out. I was sixty-five when I lost your mother. So, twelve off...how old's he now?

GEORGE Lost track. Nineteen, I suppose.

HARRY That'd make him seven. He was more than seven.

GEORGE If you say so.

HARRY He can't be nineteen then.

GEORGE I think he is, actually. He's in his second year. Birthday's in October, isn't it?

HARRY Yes, 'cause I always send him a card.

GEORGE There you are, then. *(He takes the umbrella's case from his pocket and replaces the umbrella in it.)* I don't think I'll be needing this any more today.

HARRY Forecast was good.

GEORGE Was it?

HARRY No, he was more than seven. How is that, then?

GEORGE Because...that's it, you didn't get your admission here 'til well after Mum died. You must have been sixty-six. So it's *eleven* off nineteen, not *twelve*. Eight.

HARRY Eight, then. I knew he wasn't seven.

GEORGE Who's that over there? Someone waving.

HARRY *looks.*

HARRY It's old Clarkie. *(He waves, then looks away.)* Is he coming over?

GEORGE Could be.

HARRY I can't help it if my son-in-law's working for them, can I? That's all he goes on about since he found out. On and on and on. I told him, "Change the record, Clarkie." Hasn't made a blind bit of difference.

GEORGE You're all right. He's turned off.

HARRY *looks again.*

HARRY He's going to the allotments. Half his stuff never comes up. Must be doing something, or not doing something.

GEORGE Putting carrots in again this year?

HARRY Certainly am.

GEORGE They were lovely last year.

HARRY Good.

GEORGE Delicious.

HARRY Freeze well?

GEORGE Perfect, yes.

HARRY Better make the most of them this year, then. It'll be the last. Take more than usual.

GEORGE But the allotments are staying, aren't they, for at least a year? There's no point in them putting up a...resource centre, whatever they call it, yet.

HARRY No.

GEORGE Not until they've got the car park at least, and done some of the other big stuff.

HARRY I know. Just getting a bit much. Aches and strains, boy. It comes to us all.

GEORGE Fit as a fiddle, you.

HARRY Fit to drop.

GEORGE Go on.

HARRY What do you know about it? Don't contradict your old man.

GEORGE I know how much pleasure you get from growing things over there. You might as well carry on as long as you've got the chance.

HARRY Well. It won't be the same, will it?

GEORGE What would you do instead?

HARRY I'll get my exercise, don't you worry. I've still got my keep-fit class.

GEORGE What? Oh, yes.

HARRY Thrashed Clarkie last week. Snookered him in the final frame. He wasn't best pleased.

GEORGE And you're still doing your four-forty sprint every day, down the road.

HARRY I haven't today. Thanks for reminding me. *(He dials a stored number on his phone, and passes* **GEORGE** *the newspaper, which is open at the racing page)*

GEORGE Have you got an account now?

HARRY Handy if it's raining. Engaged. Bugger it. *(He hangs up.)*

GEORGE It's not raining.

HARRY No, but I don't want to miss the three-thirty. Kempton Park. See what I've picked?

GEORGE *looks at the paper.*

GEORGE "Happy George".

HARRY I meant to go straight after my lunch. Must have dozed off.

GEORGE Too many Mackesons.

HARRY Just the one. Medicinal. They used to give it to you in hospital, years ago, bottle of stout. Good for you.

GEORGE It's the iron, I know.

HARRY It's true. "Happy George", George? Got to be worth a couple of quid. *(He redials the phone number.)*

GEORGE I shouldn't waste your money.

HARRY Bugger it. *(He hangs up, and looks at his watch.)* Don't worry, boy, I won't fritter away your inheritance. Such as it is.

GEORGE You fritter if you want to. I'm all right.

HARRY I know you're all right. That's not the point. You've got to leave something behind you. You won't do too badly, you and May.

GEORGE Yes, all well and good. I'm just saying, don't worry about spending it if you want to, as far I'm concerned. I'm sure the same goes for May.

HARRY That's not the point.

GEORGE No. I think I should be making a move.

HARRY You're not going yet?

GEORGE Could do with a pee, actually.

HARRY Nip behind the tree.

GEORGE No. I'd better be getting on.

HARRY You're going to wait and see Rupert, aren't you? Just say hello. He knows you're here.

GEORGE Behind the tree? Are you sure?

HARRY I have been known to avail myself of it before now. In dire emergencies.

GEORGE Keep a lookout then. *(He starts to move towards the tree. As he does so, he looks down at his shoes.)* These shoes are caked.

HARRY So he's doing all right then, Stefan?

GEORGE What?

HARRY Your mate.

GEORGE Bloody mud. *(Suddenly he starts to sob, inconsolably.)*

HARRY What, boy?

GEORGE I've just come from his funeral.

HARRY Dad's here. *(He puts his arm around* GEORGE *and walks him to the bench. He takes a page from the newspaper, screws it up, spits on it and starts to clean the mud from* GEORGE's *shoes.)* There's oak, and yew, and lime, and chestnut, and silver birch, and crab apple...

RUPE, *nineteen, enters. He carries a cassette recorder/ player slung over his shoulder. He stands, watching.*

...and sycamore, and monkey puzzle, and weeping willow...

HARRY *breaks off as he becomes aware of* RUPE, *who moves to the bench and places his hand on* GEORGE'*s shoulder.*

RUPE And poplar, and golden poplar, right? And dogwood, and hornbeam, and false hickory, and blue gum, and maidenhair, and snakebark maple, and tree of heaven...

Scene Two

Summer. Morning. RUPE *is sprawled on the bench.
Dressed in shorts, he has removed his shirt in the blazing
sun. He is listening to a Walkman and reading a travel
guide. He glances along the path, removes his headphones
and is putting on his shirt as* MAY, *fiftyish, enters. She
is loaded up with clothes-shop carrier bags, which she
dumps with relief.*

MAY Thank you.

RUPE What?

MAY For putting your shirt back on.

RUPE I knew you'd have a go at me if I didn't.

MAY It's Grandad. He wouldn't like you to be improperly dressed,
here.

RUPE He wouldn't mind.

MAY All right. Have it your own way.

RUPE All that walking. I'm totally wankered.

MAY I wish you wouldn't use those expressions.

RUPE Sorry.

MAY Shove up, then.

> RUPE *makes room for her to sit beside him. She removes
> a shoe and rubs her foot.*

Some idiot man trod on my foot.

RUPE Did you get what you wanted?

MAY I think I did rather well. *(She sorts through the bags and
hands some to* RUPE.*)* These are yours. Thanks for leaving
me to carry them.

RUPE You didn't give me much of a chance. You threw a moody,
just stormed off.

MAY I didn't storm off, Rupe. I wanted to have a look round Marks before it got too crowded.

RUPE I'd have come if you'd asked, right?

MAY You said you'd had enough dragging around the shops.

RUPE Yeah, right, I had. But I'd have come if you'd asked.

MAY Sometimes it's nice not to have to ask. *(She takes out a "top" from one of her bags.)* What do you think?

RUPE All right.

MAY Not too young?

RUPE Looks all right to me. You know what Dad'll say.

MAY He doesn't mean it.

RUPE "The words 'mutton' and 'lamb' spring to mind, dear."

MAY He doesn't really mean it. Did you pop in and see him?

RUPE I tried, but he was in a site meeting.

MAY I hope it doesn't go on. The table's booked for twelve-thirty. Are you going to try those trousers?

RUPE They're my size, I know. They'll be all right.

MAY I meant for lunch.

RUPE It's twenty-eight in the shade today. If we're going some place I can't wear shorts, I'm not coming.

MAY It'd just be a bit smarter. Dad won't like it.

RUPE Tough. I saw some of the second-stage drawings. This woman showed me. She was waiting for Dad. Works for the consultants, or someone.

MAY *produces a particularly vivid swimsuit from a bag.*

MAY I like this, don't you? Half price.

RUPE Couldn't you find anything brighter?

MAY Cheek! *I* like it, anyway.

RUPE The lecture theatre looks incredible. In the drawings, anyway.

MAY Oh, the chapel.

RUPE They're even using this really old wood, yeah? For the thing, the podium. And to put round the monitors and speakers and stuff.

MAY It won't much matter to Grandad, he's never been a churchgoer; but there'll be some grumbling from some of them when they have to walk along to St Barnabas. Let's hope they don't bump into any Japs.

RUPE What are you going on about?

MAY Some of the old sweats here won't take kindly to Japanese businessmen swanning around the place. Not just the Japanese, either. If that's the right word.

RUPE If what's the right word?

MAY "Swanning". Not quite right for the Japanese, somehow.

RUPE Why not?

MAY Oh, *I* don't know.

RUPE It won't be for a year or two yet, yeah?

MAY Grandad might not be here to see it.

RUPE And he might. Who knows?

MAY I'm just being realistic.

RUPE Morbid.

MAY Do you really think this is too loud?

RUPE It's all right. *You've* got to wear it. Wear what you want.

MAY Thank you. There's nothing morbid about it. When you get to Grandad's age you don't expect years and years. I was just saying that he might go before there's too many changes here.

RUPE And that'd be a good thing?

MAY Of course not. Just that it might work out like that. I was making a comment, that's all. You will keep in touch, won't you?

RUPE Yes.

MAY Postcards'll take ages I expect.

RUPE Yeah.

MAY But you'll phone?

RUPE When I can, yes. It's only four weeks.

MAY It's the other side of the world.

RUPE It might not be easy.

MAY You can reverse the charges.

RUPE No, it'll be finding one. Jen's a good five miles away from the town.

MAY The school must have one.

RUPE I'm not going to spend all my time on the phone.

MAY Just to let us know you're all right sometimes.

RUPE Right. Yes.

MAY When do you go back to Dr Willis?

RUPE Tomorrow. Last lot. *(He examines his upper arm.)* Still a bit red from last week's.

MAY You're sure he's giving you everything you need? Let's see. *(She makes as if to look at his arm.)*

RUPE It's all right. It's not sore any more.

MAY You know what he can be like.

RUPE Hepatitis, polio, typhoid, meningitis, and yellow fever. Unless you know something he doesn't, I think I'll survive, Mum, yeah?

MAY Be careful in the sun, though. You peel, you.

RUPE Better keep my shorts on for lunch, then, yeah? Acclimatization.

MAY It'll be hotter than this.

The distant clock chimes before striking twelve.

RUPE Is Uncle George going straight to the restaurant?

MAY He's coming here.

RUPE How is he?

MAY Keeping busy.

RUPE Is he very down?

MAY Of course he is. It must be hard for him.

RUPE Why don't you have him over? He could stay for a bit.

MAY I did ask.

RUPE Dad, I suppose, right?

MAY I just think he wants to be alone.

RUPE They never came over. We always used to go to them. You and me, anyway.

MAY He was a good sort, Stefan. Poor man.

RUPE I used to like going down there.

MAY Yes, you did. I'm glad you like George.

RUPE Stefan was more fun.

MAY He's always been a bit of a worrier, George.

RUPE Never liked me climbing over all that stuff in the room behind the shop.

MAY It was valuable, some of that. Very old.

RUPE I was only little. Stefan never minded. Do you remember that huge desk thing they could never sell? With the roller front business that came down, and all those bits you could pull out, and secret drawers?

MAY You shut yourself in it, one day.

RUPE Did I?

MAY Couldn't find you anywhere. You might have suffocated.

RUPE Too much woodworm for that. Stefan had a real go at Uncle George one day for telling me off about climbing on it. I was crying, and Stefan showed me all the scratches and grooves and broken bits, and made up a little story about each one, except I thought they were true.

MAY What sort of stories?

RUPE Like this one deep scratch was off a kid's silver buckle in 1791. On his shoe. And this sort of ball thing missing off one of the legs was nicked by another kid a hundred years later. So he could play Sir Francis thing and the Armada.

MAY Drake.

RUPE Right.

MAY It could well have been.

RUPE He stopped me crying. *(He looks along the path.)* Here's Grandad.

> **MAY** *waves.*

MAY He must have been at the allotments. I hope he's all right in this heat.

RUPE Did you get him a present?

MAY Sent him a card. I couldn't think of anything. He always says not to bother, anyway.

RUPE Must be baking in those trousers.

MAY Clear this stuff off, will you, there's a good boy?

> **RUPE** *replaces the clothes in the bags and clears the bench.* **MAY** *goes to greet* **HARRY** *as he enters.*

Happy birthday, Dad.

HARRY Thank you, dear. Still going strong. Rupert, how's tricks?

RUPE Good.

HARRY When are you off?

RUPE Sunday.

HARRY You look after yourself. What an adventure.

MAY I've been trying to get him to promise to phone us sometimes. Talk about a brick wall.

HARRY Do they have phones? Bush telegraph, isn't it, Rupert?

RUPE It's not exactly the jungle, Grandad.

HARRY The lad doesn't want to spend his time phoning, do you? His sister only phones birthdays and Christmas, you said.

MAY It's different for Jen. She writes every fortnight.

RUPE I'm only there four weeks.

HARRY Well, you have a good time. Enjoy yourself.

RUPE I'll send you a card.

HARRY You better. And watch out for the snakes.

MAY Oh, snakes. Don't!

RUPE Have you been at the allotment?

HARRY Yes. Just sorting out what I'm going to chuck, and what I'm going to give to Clarkie. He needs all the help he can get.

MAY I think it's a shame. You could keep it going for another year, at least.

HARRY No point, with what's going on.

MAY We'll miss your carrots, won't we, Rupe?

RUPE *I* won't. I don't like carrots.

HARRY Good for the eyesight. You...

RUPE You never see a rabbit wearing glasses. Yeah.

HARRY Well, you don't.

MAY You're not throwing out those gardening gloves from last year?

HARRY I was going to give them to Clarkie. Why? Do you want them?

MAY Well, they're still quite new, aren't they?

HARRY Hardly used. I'd rather you had them, if they'd do you a turn.

MAY Yes, please.

HARRY We'll go and get them later, before we go off. No sign of George?

MAY Not yet. We're all right though, for time.

HARRY Tell you what, Rupe, nip over and get us some ice creams. *(He gives* **RUPE** *a fiver from his pocket.)*

MAY I'll pay.

HARRY You won't. What do you want? Strawberry?

MAY Not for me. I'll spoil my lunch.

RUPE Grandad?

HARRY Anything, Rupe. Ice lolly.

RUPE Right. *(He exits.)*

MAY It *is* a bit much, isn't it, this heat?

HARRY As long as I keep in the shade.

MAY Have you seen much of Jake?

HARRY From a distance.

MAY Like me. He's always rushing off somewhere.

HARRY *You* married him.

MAY All right, Dad, I know. I never thought he'd get so, well... high-powered.

HARRY You can't hold ambition against him, May.

MAY I'm not. I'd just like to see a bit more of him. Are you still getting comments from the others?

HARRY It was only ever Clarkie. He'd eased off until he heard about the museum.

MAY What about it?

HARRY They're closing it, that's the rumour. Or putting it somewhere else, some of it. Into this resource centre when it's ready.

MAY It *is* a bit poky, that museum. And I expect there'll be lots more visitors.

HARRY It might be poky, but at least it's all out on display. They're going to put most of it into storage. All they're taking is a "selection". Sounds like a sodding box of chocolates. Just the things that fit in with the "concept", they call it. All these screens and reality displays and tape recordings, and somewhere, where it can fit in, a couple of battle honours, the most important medals, a few of the old records, and the muskets.

MAY I know. But if they're pushed for space... There *are* rows and rows of those medals. Walls full.

HARRY And they all mean something. Not just to the poor dead buggers who won them, but families. I like doing my turn in the museum. You get someone doing a bit of family research, it's interesting. The look on their faces when they can see a medal that their great-great-great-grandfather won. And why he won it. And how brave he was. Or how stupid. It's wrong to lock all that away.

MAY Won't you still be able to look after what they *are* putting on display?

HARRY Not in the same way. Not to answer questions, talk to people, show them round. They want us stuck at the entrance, like waxworks. Full ceremonial, with a partisan.

MAY A what?

HARRY Partisan. Long spear job, with a spiky, narrow blade across.

MAY Oh.

HARRY It should be a halberd for me, anyway, being a sergeant. Strictly speaking.

MAY The one with the battleaxe thing on the end?

HARRY Yes. That's what I should have. But that's not the sort of thing they worry about. It's all the same to them.

MAY You'll still get people talking to you.

HARRY Prodding us to make sure we're real, more like.

MAY Mum took George and me once.

HARRY Where?

MAY To Madame Tussauds. George gave one of the attendants a good old prod. He thought it was a dummy. He screamed when the man scratched his nose.

HARRY She was always taking you places. I'd come back on leave and you'd tell me all about it.

MAY And show you our special books. Remember? Those lovely leather-bound books with blank pages you gave us, so we could write down the places Mum took us.

HARRY Egypt, I got them.

MAY Wonder where they are now?

HARRY George has got them.

MAY Mine as well? After all these years?

HARRY That's what he told me, a couple of years back.

MAY Well I never. I'd love to see them.

HARRY Ask him. Have you been down...since?

MAY I offered.

HARRY I hope he's looking after himself.

MAY I'll keep an eye on him. He sounded a bit brighter when I spoke to him about today.

HARRY Thanks, May.

MAY You do know you can always come to us, don't you? I mean as a permanent thing, if you really can't stand all these changes.

HARRY No, no, no.

MAY The offer's there if you want it. I've talked it over with Jake. We've got the room.

HARRY I'm here because I want to be. It's a good place to come and die.

MAY Dad.

HARRY It was the saving of me, coming here. I want for nothing.

MAY But all these changes.

HARRY I'll live with them, don't you worry. We'll have to.

MAY Well, if you ever feel you can't...

Unnoticed by either of them until it collides with MAY's *ankle, a large radio-controlled model JCB excavator zooms along the path.* MAY *screams.* HARRY *picks up the truck and calls off.*

HARRY Where's your L-plates, Craig?

MAY That hurt.

HARRY *(to* MAY*)* Clarkie's great-grandson. *(calling off)* Hello, Maureen.

MAY Ow.

HARRY *places the JCB back on the path and it zooms back where it came from.* HARRY *waves.*

HARRY Spoilt little... Are you all right?

MAY Just.

HARRY One thing about Rupert. You never spoiled him.

MAY No.

HARRY He's got a head on his shoulders. You shouldn't worry about him.

MAY He likes his home comforts, though.

HARRY Do him good to rough it for a change.

MAY Honestly, the letters from Jen about the conditions out there. There's no running water where she is, and they keep having these blackouts. Electricity failures, generators going wrong all the time. He likes his shower, Rupe. She has to fill up this tin bath, out on the verandah. Well I showed you her last lot of photos.

HARRY Happy as Larry, she looked, surrounded by all those kids.

MAY They have to share six books between forty of them in her class. I don't know how she manages.

HARRY Anyway, it never did *you* any harm.

MAY What didn't?

HARRY Using a tin bath.

MAY Oh, the old house, yes. In the kitchen. Mum heating up the copper and then ladling the water in with that huge saucepan. *(She shudders.)* Ooh!

HARRY What?

MAY It just came back to me. Catching a toe-nail on the side. Like scratching a dustbin or a blackboard. Horrid. Oh, and the outside toilet.

HARRY It served its purpose. It was only just outside. Wasn't as if you had to go right up the end of the garden.

MAY It felt far enough in winter. When I look back... Jake thought I was kidding when we first met, about that toilet.

HARRY How is he now, about Jen?

MAY I think he's got used to it.

HARRY He should be proud of her.

MAY At least he's stopped calling her a "do-gooder". He does annoy me sometimes. Rupe can't do anything wrong, and Jen can't do anything right. I'm sure he half hopes Rupe going over to see her will make her come back and think about doing something more... "solid", he'd call it. It's costing a fortune.

HARRY You can afford it. A once in a lifetime thing. It's a good chance for him.

MAY You're a bit behind the times, Dad. They go off at the drop of a hat these days, to the ends of the earth. It's not the money. Jake wants him to pay it back, anyway, once he gets a job. I think he was joking. I hope he was.

HARRY It's a year to go, is that right? For Rupert? I was trying to remember the other day.

MAY This time next year, yes. If he doesn't have to do any re-sits.

HARRY He'll sail through.

MAY He's not really been buckling down to it this year. I don't know why.

HARRY He's never failed an exam yet, has he? He'll do fine.

MAY I just hope there's a job for him at the end of it all.

HARRY Last time I saw Jake he seemed to think things were on the up. They always need good people in personnel.

MAY You *are* behind the times. "Human Resource Management".

HARRY Whatever they call it, it's still a good job.

MAY And so's what Jen's doing. I wish he'd see it that way. A different sort of good. "Marching to a different drummer", or however that thing goes.

HARRY Stand up to him. You've got a right to your opinions.

MAY You stop believing you have an opinion if nobody listens to you.

   GEORGE *enters.*

GEORGE Happy birthday.

HARRY There you are, boy.

MAY Hello, George dear.

GEORGE How's things?

MAY Not too bad.

HARRY Good journey?

GEORGE Fine.

HARRY Roads not too busy?

GEORGE I got the train. *(to* **MAY***)* Been hitting the sales, I see. Going drastic with the plastic.

MAY Not drastic, no. I got some bargains though.

GEORGE You always do.

HARRY Got your card. Very near the knuckle.

GEORGE Did it give you a laugh?

HARRY Oh, *I* laughed. Showed it to Clarkie, he was a bit shocked. Said he was.

MAY Oh, yes?

HARRY You don't want to know, May.

GEORGE It wasn't that bad, Dad. *(He reaches in a pocket and produces an envelope which he gives to* **HARRY***.)* I forgot to put these in. Theatre tickets.

HARRY Thank you, boy.

MAY That's nice.

HARRY What for?

GEORGE Well, not tickets, vouchers, so you needn't look so worried. You can choose what you want to see.

MAY Oh dear, yes. Last time. *(to* **HARRY***)* When Stefan was bad and George had those tickets.

HARRY No point pretending I was enjoying it if I wasn't.

GEORGE No. Fine.

HARRY Not my idea of a good play. All doom and gloom.

GEORGE Well...

HARRY This gloomy Danish lot carrying on, up to all sorts.

GEORGE Norwegian.

HARRY Scandinavian, anyway.

MAY That's Hamlet, Dad.

HARRY What is?

MAY Gloomy Dane.

HARRY He couldn't be gloomier than this lot. Not their fault. It's their weather, being in the dark most of the year.

MAY Yes. I'd hate that.

HARRY I said to him, "A bit of decent sunshine and they'd soon cheer up."

GEORGE Announced to the rest of the dress circle, I think, rather than said to me.

HARRY I wasn't that loud. Don't exaggerate. Gave them a laugh though, didn't it?

GEORGE Yes.

HARRY More than they were getting off the play.

GEORGE Yes. Where's Rupe?

MAY He went to get some ice creams. How have you been, then?

GEORGE All right.

MAY Really?

HARRY *(to* **GEORGE***)* Do you want one, ice cream? *(He stands up.)*

MAY We can send Rupe back. He won't mind.

HARRY No, I'll stroll over, meet him halfway. *(to* **GEORGE***)* What do you want?

GEORGE Anything. Are you sure you want to make the effort in this heat?

HARRY Don't fuss. See you in a minute. *(He exits.)*

MAY You're still not driving?

GEORGE I tried the other day, just down to the village. I had to turn round and come back.

MAY Give it time, dear. It's only been four months.

GEORGE Other things are all right. That's not strictly true. But I suppose bursting into tears and shaking and not being able to control it, at least it isn't dangerous if it happens in the shop. Just embarrassing when there's a customer in.

MAY I still think you opened up again too soon.

GEORGE I had to do something. Have a reason to get up, start a routine again.

MAY Did you go to the doctor?

GEORGE I thought about it.

MAY And?

GEORGE I decided against.

MAY You could get something to sleep, at least.

GEORGE I don't want to be groggy all day.

MAY They must have things now. You like that doctor, don't you?

GEORGE She was wonderful with Stefan, yes.

MAY Well, then. Just go and see her, have a little chat about things.

GEORGE It's natural, what I'm going through. That's what everyone says. I think I should just let things take their course, not start popping pills at my age.

MAY At your age? Go on.

GEORGE I'm feeling old, May.

MAY You're feeling sad. The two don't necessarily go together.

GEORGE I suppose not. You're usually right, aren't you?

MAY I try my best.

GEORGE I mean, look at Dad. He never seems sad.

MAY Angry, at the moment.

GEORGE Is he?

MAY I think, generally, yes. About all the changes here.

GEORGE Good for him. I would be.

MAY Jake says they're bringing some of it forward.

GEORGE Why?

MAY It's to do with drainage or something. They'll have to start here sooner than they thought.

GEORGE The gardens?

MAY Yes. Digging all this up. It's a shame.

GEORGE How much sooner?

MAY Early next year. January, he reckons. It means he's got to work twice the hours. More trips.

GEORGE What, Frankfurt?

MAY I don't know why they can't come over here for a change.

GEORGE Nearer for the Swiss, I suppose. How often does he go over?

MAY I lose track. I'd have to count the bottles of perfume. Duty frees.

GEORGE I like the one you've got on. Very summery.

MAY The Swiss, the Germans, the Japanese. Call me old-fashioned...

GEORGE You're old-fashioned.

MAY Well...especially somewhere like this.

GEORGE What do you expect? Money's international. Who owns your water now, or your electricity? Do you know?

MAY Don't get all political or we'll row.

GEORGE It *is*.

MAY It's just a feeling. Some things are. It doesn't *feel* right.

GEORGE *looks along the path.*

GEORGE He was quick.

MAY Rupe must have been nearly back.

The clock chimes the quarter hour.

Now he'll have to go all the way over again. Where's Jake? I hope he's not going to be late.

HARRY *enters. He has two ice lollies and a can of coke.*

Did you send Rupe back?

HARRY No, he's just round the corner. We got ambushed by Clarkie and his lot. I said I better get these back before they melt. *(to GEORGE)* Strawberry thing with ice cream in the middle, or a plain orange?

GEORGE Orange'll do. Thanks.

Both men unwrap their lollies and start to eat them.

HARRY He'd got himself a drink as well, anyway, so he's happy with that, he says. Unless you'd rather have it, and he'll have the lolly.

GEORGE This is fine.

MAY Let's have a taste.

HARRY I thought you didn't want to spoil your lunch.

MAY Just a nibble, see what it's like.

HARRY As the bombardier said to the tart.

MAY Dad! *(She tries* **GEORGE***'s lolly and hands it back.)* Lovely.

HARRY Try some strawberry?

MAY No, thank you.

GEORGE I'm surprised it's not busier here today.

HARRY Too hot. Nobody wants to just sit when it's this hot nowadays. It's all take everything off and sprawl about. They'll be over the park. That'll be packed.

MAY I don't like parks any more. Those dogs.

GEORGE You like dogs, don't you?

MAY Not the ones you get now. You're afraid to even look at them. I half expect them to say something if I catch their eye: "What are you looking at?" *(to* **HARRY***)* Go on then. Just to taste. *(She tries* **HARRY***'s lolly.)*

GEORGE Careful, it's dripping.

MAY Oh, no. Damnation. Where's my handbag? Quick. Handbag. *(She hands the lolly back to* **HARRY***.)*

GEORGE *(à la Lady Bracknell)* Your handbag?

MAY Come on, quick.

HARRY It's only a bit. Hardly notices.

GEORGE Under your feet.

> **MAY** *takes a tissue from her bag and dabs at the spot.*

HARRY You can hardly see it.

MAY Making it worse.

GEORGE You can't really see it, May.

HARRY Leave it. *We* don't mind.

MAY *I* mind, Dad. *I* mind, thank you. And I'm the one wearing it. So I can mind if I want to.

She wets the tissue with her tongue and dabs away.
RUPE *enters.*

GEORGE Hello, Rupe.

RUPE All right, Uncle George?

GEORGE Good to see you. Bit of a drippy lolly crisis.

MAY *(to* **RUPE***)* I expect you were dawdling. They wouldn't be half melted if you weren't.

RUPE You said you didn't want one.

MAY I didn't. I was just having a taste.

HARRY The strawberry one.

GEORGE The flavour is immaterial.

HARRY What?

RUPE There's nothing there, Mum. You can't see it.

MAY I'll scream in a minute.

HARRY You need water on it. That's what you need. Come on.

MAY Where?

HARRY There's a tap at the allotments.

MAY Worth a try, I suppose.

HARRY We'll pick up those gardening gloves at the same time.

MAY *(to* **RUPE***)* No sign of Dad yet?

RUPE No.

HARRY *and* **MAY** *exit.*

Just as well. He'll get an earful of Clarkie if he turns up now.

GEORGE Having a go at you, was he?

RUPE Well gutted, he is. Thought he was going to burst something.

GEORGE Do you ever talk to him about what's going on here? Your dad.

RUPE A bit, sometimes. It's quite interesting, I suppose. The designs and stuff.

GEORGE Whatever happened to your plans about going into something like that?

RUPE When?

GEORGE I don't mean buildings, specifically. Design generally though. You used to have those projects from school and we'd go over them when you came down. Furniture was your thing.

RUPE Still got the drawings somewhere.

GEORGE You had some good ideas.

RUPE Stefan liked them, yeah.

GEORGE So did I.

RUPE Too modern, you said.

GEORGE Did I?

RUPE Yeah.

GEORGE I do like a chair to be a chair, yes. Something you can sit in comfortably without feeling you're an exhibit.

RUPE Right. Too modern.

GEORGE Not necessarily. The principles don't change. Yours were good. Construction, materials.

RUPE I suppose I got that from watching you restore stuff.

GEORGE You just lost interest, or what?

RUPE I suppose. Anyway, it's too uncertain, isn't it? To do that, like as a career.

GEORGE What *isn't*?

RUPE At least I'll have a properly defined career structure.

GEORGE God, that sounds like your father. Does he talk about the "world of work" as well?

RUPE He has, yeah.

GEORGE Always sounds like a theme park to me. Sorry. None of my business.

RUPE He's done all right for himself.

GEORGE Oh, yes. No, good luck to him. He's doing what he wants. Nothing wrong with that.

RUPE Right.

GEORGE Career comes from the French. The word.

RUPE Yeah?

GEORGE *"Carrière"*. A racecourse. Careering around. Trying to be first past the post.

RUPE Right.

GEORGE Anyway. All ready for Sunday, are you? Packed?

RUPE Not taking much. Won't need it.

GEORGE Send me a card.

RUPE Course.

    GEORGE *takes a fountain pen from his pocket and hands it to* **RUPE**.

GEORGE You can write it with this.

RUPE I've got pens.

GEORGE Look at it. In the top of the cap.

RUPE Oh yeah. Excellent. It's a little compass.

GEORGE In case you get lost. It was Stefan's. There's so much stuff.

RUPE Thanks, Uncle George.

GEORGE Rupe, will you do something for me?

RUPE What?

GEORGE Stop calling me Uncle George. Don't you think it's time?

RUPE Yeah, if you like...Uncle George.

GEORGE Very funny.

RUPE Why?

GEORGE Why do you think?

RUPE It makes you feel old?

GEORGE In one. From someone of your age, yes, it does.

RUPE You *are*. A bit.

GEORGE Thank you.

RUPE "George", right.

GEORGE Right. Do you really think of me as old?

RUPE I *think* of you as Uncle George. I suppose that'll change. Not because of what I call you. But me getting older.

GEORGE You didn't answer the question.

RUPE What is "old", yeah? But, no, last Christmas?

GEORGE What?

RUPE The CD you gave me. *Supertramp*?

GEORGE You said you liked it.

RUPE I did. It was the dog's bollocks.

GEORGE Oh, good.

RUPE No, it was when I was skipping through the tracks trying to find that song you wanted me to hear. You said, "Perhaps it's on the other side, turn it over."

GEORGE I didn't.

RUPE You did, George.

GEORGE You didn't say anything.

RUPE I told Stefan. He pissed himself.

GEORGE Not literally, I hope.

RUPE No. Are you all right about all that?

GEORGE Sort of. The first time I felt old was this party, ten years ago. I was introduced to a boy...man...about your age. Dylan. I said, "Oh? Your parents like poetry? Are they Welsh?" Total blank. "Dylan Thomas." "Who? No, they called me after some old singer." Please say you get it, Rupe, or I'll feel a hundred and nine.

RUPE Sorry about the funeral.

GEORGE I'm glad your mother was there.

RUPE I didn't fancy it really.

GEORGE Doesn't matter.

RUPE I sort of felt I'd said goodbye. I went to see him. In his last week.

GEORGE Did you? He never said.

RUPE It was a bit private.

GEORGE Oh, yes?

RUPE We talked about stuff.

GEORGE Stuff?

RUPE Things I couldn't talk to Mum and Dad about.

GEORGE You could have come to me.

RUPE That wasn't why I went to see him. It just came out, somehow. He started to ask things.

GEORGE Typical Stefan. He never could concentrate on the matter in hand, like dying.

HARRY and MAY enter. She carries a pair of gardening gloves.

MAY This heat. Dad had to have a sit down.

GEORGE *(to HARRY)* You're all right?

HARRY Stop fussing. I'm AI.

MAY Where's Jake?

GEORGE No sign of him yet.

MAY It's twenty-five past, nearly. *(to GEORGE, indicating her dress)* That's all right now, isn't it?

GEORGE Can't see a thing, honestly.

MAY *(to RUPE)* Are you sure you're going to stay in those shorts?

RUPE Yeah.

MAY Are you all right now, Dad?

HARRY Yes.

MAY *You* don't mind, do you?

HARRY What?

MAY Rupe's coming like that, in his shorts.

RUPE Stop going on.

MAY I'm not going on. Just asking.

HARRY Makes no odds to me. They can be a bit toffee-nosed in that place, though.

MAY There you are, Rupe.

HARRY No. You wear what you like, boy. *(to MAY)* Nobody'll see once he's sat down.

RUPE *(to* MAY*)* Yeah. All right?

GINNY *(offstage)* Hello?

They all look along the path.

MAY Who's that?

RUPE It's the woman who showed me the plans.

GEORGE Who?

RUPE Coming over. I saw her this morning, waiting for Dad.

MAY Smart outfit.

HARRY Who is she?

MAY Something to do with the alterations.

HARRY That's one word for it.

GINNY *(offstage)* Rupert. Hello again.

RUPE All right?

GINNY, *mid-thirties, enters. She carries a briefcase.*

GINNY Hello. You must be Mrs Dickinson. And that'll be your father. Happy birthday!

HARRY Yes, thanks.

GINNY I'm Ginny.

MAY This is George, my brother.

GINNY Hello. I'm afraid I bring disappointment. Your husband says he's not going to be able to make lunch.

MAY Oh.

GINNY Not for twelve-thirty, anyway. He might get along for a drink later, he said.

HARRY Never mind, May.

MAY Have to go without him then.

GINNY Enjoy yourselves.

MAY Thank you. Carry some of these bags, will you, Rupe?

RUPE *starts to gather the carrier bags.* GEORGE *helps.*

GINNY Oh, I don't know if you're aware of it, but have you spilt something? There...a sort of pinkish damp patch.

MAY Yes. Thank you.

GEORGE Let's go then.

HARRY *(to* GINNY*)* What do *you* do for them?

GINNY P.R. Public relations, yes?

HARRY Yes.

GEORGE You must have your work cut out.

GINNY It's a challenge. *(She sits on the bench and puts her briefcase beside her.)*

HARRY Where do you have *your* lunch?

GINNY I don't if I can help it. I have to with clients, of course. I'm not really a lunch person though.

HARRY Thought you might have sandwiches in there.

GEORGE Ready, Dad?

GINNY Oh, no.

HARRY Because it's no picnicking in these gardens. Tell people, they argue the toss sometimes.

GINNY No sandwiches. Promise. Just work to catch up on in these beautiful surroundings. *(She looks in the direction of the building.)* Look, *there's* Mr Dickinson, I think, waving from that window. The second floor.

The others follow her gaze. GEORGE *gives a desultory wave,* MAY *an exaggerated shrug.*

GEORGE Come on, then.

GINNY *moves with them as they go to exit.*

MAY Nice meeting you.

GINNY You too, Mrs Dickinson. Goodbye.

RUPE 'Bye.

HARRY, GEORGE, RUPE *and* **MAY** *exit.*

GINNY Have a marvellous time.

MAY *(offstage)* Thank you. 'Bye.

> GINNY *watches them go, then goes back to a spot from where she can see the building. She looks in the same direction as before but sees nothing. She opens her briefcase, takes out a small mirror and adjusts her hair. She takes out two glasses and places them on the bench. She takes out a half bottle of champagne, testing its coolness against her cheek before easing out the cork. The model JCB reappears, moving along the path past her. She watches it disappear, then starts to fill the glasses.*

ACT TWO

Scene One

Autumn. Morning. (Everyone except RUPE *wears a
remembrance poppy.)* GINNY *enters briskly. She carries
a camera bag which she puts down on the bench. As
she takes a camcorder from the bag she looks off and
calls out.*

GINNY Not too fast, I want to get you in the distance first. *(She
points the camcorder and operates it.)* Can you possibly stop
and look around at the trees...yes, lovely...and a cheery little
wave...no, not at the camera, to those two other residents,
on the main path...yes, lovely. I'm coming in close on you
now, so just carry on normally...

We hear the sound of an approaching helicopter.

...perhaps stop for a second and look over towards the gate...
and then on...lovely...

*She looks up as the helicopter is passing overhead, and
follows it with the camera.* HARRY, *walking now with
a stick, enters as the noise from the helicopter is at its
loudest. He speaks, but we can't hear what he's saying.
As the noise fades,* GINNY *stops filming.*

Sorry?

HARRY I was saying, does it ever make you think? That sort
of noise. About long ago.

GINNY I'm not quite with you.

HARRY The loudest thing someone would have heard. When I
was a lad it was a steam train. I never imagined anything

could be louder than that. My father too, I suppose, before the big field guns when he joined up. *His* father...machinery, I suppose, in the factory. Or the factory whistle giving a blast.

GINNY Things *are* getting noisier all round, aren't they? Even in the countryside.

HARRY Thunder, years and years ago, that's the loudest they'd have heard. All their lives.

GINNY I suppose so, yes. Honestly, where my parents live now, I mean it's miles from anywhere, but it's never completely quiet.

HARRY See them a lot, do you?

GINNY Quite often, yes. When I can get down there.

HARRY George and May are very good. They come quite a lot.

GINNY That's nice. Actually I'm going down later, after I've watched the parade.

HARRY Filming that too, are you?

GINNY Yes. I thought I'd get a good view from here.

HARRY Who's it for, then? Who do you show it to?

GINNY Oh, it's just for me. Later on, we'll get a proper video made, show the work in progress and so on. For the investors. This is just for me, so I can sort of soak up the atmosphere, get a feel for the place, think about how we might reposition it.

HARRY Move it?

GINNY Sorry, you misunderstand. Reposition it in people's perception. What it was, and what it will become.

HARRY Oh, I see. Going to say, even Jake hasn't mentioned *moving* it.

GINNY No.

HARRY Digging up these gardens, some new buildings, tearing the heart out of the old ones, but not actually *moving* them.

GINNY No. So does your family always come for today?

HARRY Oh, yes. Well, not my grandson every year, but he's coming today. Jake won't be here though. He's had to go off.

GINNY He mentioned it, yes.

HARRY Frankfurt.

GINNY Is it? I take it you'll be putting on your smart red coat for the parade?

HARRY We don't wear red coats.

GINNY Surely you do. I mean I just saw your lieutenant *(She pronounces it "lootenant".)* chap. He was wearing one.

HARRY The lieutenant-governor?

GINNY That's the one. I asked if he wanted to tag along with me, so I could get some nice shots of him, but he didn't seem very keen.

HARRY It's scarlet. Red is for pillar boxes. And robins.

GINNY I must remember that. Scarlet. Thank you. There's such a lot, isn't there? All this tradition.

HARRY I don't put mine on 'til the last minute. Just before we muster.

GINNY A bit uncomfortable, I expect. Scratchy?

HARRY It's not that.

GINNY What, then?

HARRY Difficult to explain.

GINNY Sorry. I didn't mean to pry.

The clock chimes the half hour.

HARRY No.

GINNY Well, I think perhaps I should get some more stuff down near the allotments. *(She picks up the camcorder and* *points it at* **HARRY***.)* Could I just do a really big close-up of you? I'm trying to get lots of faces. Faces are lovely for me.

HARRY Good job I'm not in one of those tribes.

GINNY Sorry?

HARRY Like you always see, you know. Primitive tribes. You can't take a picture of them because it steals away their spirit. That sort of old tosh.

GINNY Well, if they believe it...who are we?

HARRY Almost got my throat cut once, taking a photo. When I was in the desert. These bedouins. We'd got lost, my patrol, and we ran into their camp. Very friendly, hospitable, gave us some water. They didn't like the Germans any more than we did, or that's what they said, anyway. I wandered off, oh, a hundred yards, other side of a dune, and there was this really beautiful young lass squatting on her haunches in the sand, perfectly still...what's the word? ...serene, perfectly serene, long white djellaba, robe thing they wear, just staring into the distance. And I had this first-class Leica round my neck that I'd...liberated, and it was such a good picture, I had to get it, and I'd focussed and everything and I was just about to take it when she looked over and saw me. Talk about a scream. Went right through me. More like a wailing. Terrible noise. Next thing I know they're all round me jabbering away and I've got a knife at my throat, wicked big curved job, and the lads arrive with their rifles, and it all calms down eventually, smiles all round, misunderstanding, no offence meant. Near thing though.

GINNY Lucky you. But I suppose in their culture you *were* sort of stealing something. I do think we have to be sensitive to things like that.

HARRY Oh, it wasn't that. It was only when she jumped up I realized. She'd been having a...going to the toilet.

GINNY Oh.

HARRY No wonder she didn't like it. You wouldn't, would you?

GINNY No.

HARRY I'll never forget seeing that. Lying there in all its glory. Steaming. I laughed, of course, which made things worse.

GINNY Your son-in-law said you had lots of stories.

HARRY Did he?

GINNY Yes.

HARRY I don't think he believes half of them.

GINNY No?

HARRY I think he thinks I'm teasing him.

GINNY Are you teasing me?

HARRY I don't know you. I wouldn't tease people I don't know.

GINNY I'm sorry if you really do think we're tearing the heart out. That's not the intention. It's in no one's interest to lose the essential character of this place. Quite the reverse. That's what people will be coming for. An oasis, if you like, of solid values, of a sense of the past, continuity. Why shouldn't other people share in that?

HARRY You think I'm being selfish?

GINNY Not selfish. Perhaps a little, yes, actually, if you don't mind my saying so.

HARRY Be my guest.

GINNY And that's just what people will be. Guests.

HARRY Paying guests.

GINNY Have you any idea what it costs to get a conference centre up and running? Especially here, with all the constraints of planning and preservation. A lot of people have worked jolly hard, you know, to make sure everyone's views are taken into account. I think we've achieved a good balance. The best of the old, safely nestling in the strength of the new, that's how I like to think of it.

HARRY I read, yes.

GINNY I have the greatest respect, you know, for history, tradition. I'm no philistine.

HARRY I never said you were.

GINNY Only you'd think I was, judging from some people's attitude. I mean they never seem to consider the benefits. If one believes that a place has a heart, a spirit or whatever, then that can benefit everyone. I like to think, perhaps fancifully you'd say, I expect, that if there's some hugely important conference here, say medical, trying to get to grips with cancer or whatever, that the doctors might come to better decisions. They'll be in the right frame of mind. At ease with themselves. It might even help them make a breakthrough. Silly perhaps, I know, but that's what I think.

HARRY You don't have to convince me. I'll just do what I'm told. Orders.

GINNY But you have a right to understand.

HARRY I do.

GINNY Are you sure?

HARRY Quite sure.

GINNY A hundred percent?

HARRY As near as dammit is to swearing.

GINNY Good. I do want people to understand, you see. I'm very relieved.

HARRY Talking of which, I've just got to strain the greens.

GINNY Sorry?

HARRY Behind the tree. I'm bursting.

GINNY I see.

> **HARRY** *disappears behind the tree.* **GINNY** *replaces the camcorder in its bag.*

HARRY Keep a lookout.

GINNY Oh. Yes.

HARRY All clear?

GINNY Yes.

HARRY It's a sturdy old tree, this.

GINNY Yes.

HARRY Look at those branches. Even the smallest ones. Thick as a darkie's todger.

GINNY Sorry? Darkest what?

> GEORGE *enters, unnoticed by* GINNY, *who has turned to look at the tree. He has a small carrier bag.*

You see, I think we should embrace change. I don't think we should be afraid of it. I'm sure once you get used to it… I know you're in your seniority now, but growth is still important, don't you think, however old one is? And I'm sure you've got a good few years in you yet. *(She suddenly becomes aware of* GEORGE.*)*

GEORGE Sorry to startle you. I didn't want to interrupt your conversation.

GINNY I didn't see you coming.

GEORGE A bit one-sided, I would have thought.

GINNY What? Oh, no…

> HARRY *emerges from behind the tree.*

HARRY Hello, boy.

GEORGE Ah.

GINNY You didn't really think I was…

GEORGE Hello, Dad. *(to* GINNY*)* No. Well, just for a second. You don't seem the type.

GINNY No.

HARRY Good journey?

GEORGE Fine.

GINNY I must get on. Excuse me.

HARRY Won't put *you* on sentry duty again.

GINNY Thank you. *(She exits.)*

GEORGE Have you been giving her a hard time?

HARRY Me? No.

GEORGE Not the brightest of women.

HARRY About as bright as a shilling up a sweep's arse. What have you got there?

GEORGE It's for May. It's her book. Remember I kept them?

GEORGE hands the bag to HARRY who opens it and takes out the book.

HARRY Yes, she was asking me.

GEORGE She'd forgotten I'd kept them.

HARRY Good bit of tooling, that. Very intricate.

GEORGE Egyptian?

HARRY Alex, yes. Alexandria. In the market.

GEORGE "Souk", you used to call it.

HARRY "Souk", yes, that's it.

GEORGE Have a glance through. There's some lovely stuff in there; May when she was young, writing all these long, long descriptions of where we'd been, to tell you.

HARRY Another time. I'll let *her* show me.

GEORGE She wouldn't mind.

HARRY No. I've read it anyway. *(He replaces the book in the bag.)*

GEORGE Not for years.

HARRY There's nothing wrong with my memory.

GEORGE I didn't say there was.

HARRY I've still got my full complement of marbles, boy. My memory doesn't need nudging.

GEORGE No. It's not that. I just thought you might like a look.

HARRY Glad to hear it. There's always someone trying nowadays. I'm AI in that department. We had this thing the other week. "Memory Workshop". Voluntary, but I gave it a look in, just to see.

GEORGE "Never volunteer".

HARRY You'd think I'd have learnt by now, wouldn't you? These two lasses with old photos and newspapers and question after question, even when you didn't have anything to say. And a singalong at the end. Vera Lynn medley. I hate bloody Vera Lynn. Never could stand her.

GEORGE Who *did* you like, then? If you remember?

HARRY Bit of respect, you. You sent me a postcard from Alexandria.

GEORGE Yes.

HARRY When you were on holiday with Stefan.

GEORGE Yes.

HARRY I don't think I ever said thank you.

GEORGE Didn't you?

HARRY I should have seen more of him. Got to know him better.

GEORGE Got to know him at all.

HARRY Yes. I'm sorry.

GEORGE No. It doesn't matter, honestly.

HARRY Sure?

GEORGE Yes.

HARRY Thank you.

GEORGE May said Rupe's coming.

HARRY Yes, but not Jake.

GEORGE I'm glad she's got Rupe. Glad you've got grandchildren.

HARRY He's a good lad.

GEORGE Did you get a card from him?

HARRY Yes. Jen put a bit too. He said it was all very smelly, but nice smells, some of them. Spices, in the market.

GEORGE Mine said he'd had a bit of an adventure, whatever that means.

HARRY Didn't say what?

GEORGE Said he'd tell me about it when he saw me. *(He looks at his watch.)* May's usually here by now, isn't she? Shouldn't you be getting ready?

HARRY I'm all right for a bit. I'd like to see them before, just say hello.

GEORGE Traffic, I expect. Busy for a Sunday, coming in from me, anyway. Think it'll stay fine?

HARRY Hope so.

GEORGE It was a real Indian summer, wasn't it?

HARRY She gets on my nerves, that's all.

GEORGE Who? Oh.

HARRY Poncing around like Lady Muck. I try to be polite, but it's an uphill bloody struggle sometimes. They don't understand anything, any of them. Don't even try, if you ask me. Never mind all the meetings and what have you, consultations.

GEORGE Don't tell me. Tell her.

HARRY I had to bite my tongue just now.

GEORGE Don't then.

HARRY Well. *(He stands up and moves around the back of the tree, looking up.)* And that's still there.

GEORGE What?

HARRY Plastic bag, caught in that branch.

GEORGE *joins him.*

Been there for days. *(He reaches upwards with his walking stick at arm's length.)*

GEORGE You won't get it with that. It's too high.

HARRY Only just. I can try. *(He continues reaching up with the stick.)*

GEORGE You won't get it like that.

HARRY *starts to bang the stick against the bough.*

Dad.

HARRY I hate plastic bags in trees. They stay there getting all manky and dirty... *(He bangs with increasing frustrated ferocity.)*

GEORGE Easy does it, Dad. That won't do it. You'll break it.

HARRY Try this then. *(He throws the stick upwards. It falls back to the ground.)* Almost.

GEORGE Dad.

HARRY Try again. *(He throws the stick up and again it falls to the ground.)*

GEORGE It'll stay up there if you're not careful. Then where will you be?

HARRY *tries again.*

HARRY I don't need the thing. Only took it to keep the quack happy.

GINNY *enters.* **HARRY** *leaves the stick where it falls.*

GINNY Conkers?

HARRY What?

GINNY I wondered what you were doing.

HARRY Wrong sort of tree.

GEORGE You were quick.

GINNY Yes. Not a huge success, I'm afraid. *(to* **HARRY***)* One of your comrades was a bit off with me. Little man. Big eyebrows, hairy ears.

GEORGE Clarkie. What did he say?

GINNY I won't repeat it, if you don't mind. It was rather horrid.

HARRY Rude, was he?

GINNY Obscene, actually.

HARRY Sounds like him. Understandable, though, just a bit, don't you think?

GINNY Sorry?

HARRY Not the obscenity, no. No call for that. But if you will go trampling round like you're on safari, trying to film us like we're some kind of weird and wonderful wildlife, what do you expect?

GINNY I don't expect to be spoken to like *he* did. That's not what I'm doing, anyway. I thought I'd explained to you. I thought you understood.

GEORGE He does.

HARRY That's why I don't put my coat on 'til the last minute. Wear that, and all people see, some people, is what *you* see. Pomp and circumstance. And that's all right, I mean, I'll do all that because it goes with this place. But it's not everything, it's not even the most important thing. Do you think I need today to remember? The music and the marching and the showing off?

GINNY Look, I'm sorry if I said something...

HARRY *I* remember the glorious dead, poor buggers, every day of my life. And I'll be another poor bugger, I expect, before too long, and I hope it's before you and your kind take over. "Sacred and Intire", that's what our Charter says. "Given to a use so pious of itself, so honourable to the publick, it shall always be preserved Sacred and Intire."

GINNY It will stay sacred. Perhaps not entire, I grant you, but we can't expect the public purse to fund nostalgia, not these days.

HARRY It's not nostalgia. *(to* **GEORGE***)* Tell May and Rupe I'll see them after. I'm going to put on my scarlet. *(to* **GINNY***)* It's our lives.

   HARRY *exits.* **GEORGE** *picks up the walking stick and calls after him.*

GEORGE Dad.

HARRY *(offstage)* Leave it.

GEORGE "Past salvation."

GINNY Sorry?

GEORGE Family joke. We were in the park, and this kid came up and asked if he was Salvation Army. "Army, yes, but I'm past salvation, son."

GINNY I really didn't mean to upset your father.

GEORGE I don't think you did. Mean to.

GINNY I'm sorry.

GEORGE Yes.

GINNY He wasn't serious, was he, about not being with us too much longer?

GEORGE I hope not. I don't think so.

GINNY He seems in good health for his age.

GEORGE Wouldn't tell me, I don't think, anyway, if he could possibly avoid it.

GINNY I hate dying.

GEORGE I beg your pardon?

GINNY Thinking about it. I know we've all got to do it eventually, but I don't like thinking about it.

GEORGE I don't think anyone *likes* to, exactly.

GINNY I can't stop myself sometimes. All I can do then is to try and take the long-term view on it.

GEORGE Very wise.

GINNY I suppose that option's not available to your father.

GEORGE The trouble with dying is it leaves you so bloody stiff next morning.

GINNY Sorry? Oh, you're teasing. You're just like your father.

GEORGE Good.

GINNY I hate being teased. It was always the first step to bullying at school.

GEORGE You're not being teased.

GINNY I do believe in what I'm doing.

GEORGE Honestly? Deep down?

GINNY Yes.

GEORGE I never thought I *was* like him, for all sorts of reasons, but I'm glad someone else can see it. Especially you. Thank you.

GINNY Not at all. I gather you lost your...friend, recently.

GEORGE That's right.

GINNY Mr Dickinson mentioned it.

GEORGE Did he?

GINNY In passing. I'm very sorry.

GEORGE Thank you.

GINNY Had he...known, for long? Only, as a matter of fact, I've got a cousin who's...

GEORGE Twenty-one years ago, he was diagnosed.

GINNY Twenty-one years? Surely that's not possible. I always understood it was...that's wonderful to hear.

GEORGE What? Oh, I see. Stefan had MS. Multiple sclerosis, yes?

GINNY Yes. I'm sorry, I just assumed, you know...

GEORGE We do die of other things.

The clock chimes the three-quarter hour.

GINNY I must just dash to the loo, actually.

GEORGE There's always the tree.

GINNY I don't think so. Mind that, would you, if you'd be so kind, for the moment?

She indicates the camera bag and exits. **GEORGE** *goes to the tree, places both hands on the trunk and looks up into the branches.* **RUPE** *enters.*

RUPE You'll get stuck. Fire brigade time, yeah?

GEORGE What? Hello, Rupe.

RUPE All right, George?

GEORGE Fine, yes. Welcome back. Thanks for the card.

RUPE Right.

GEORGE Where's May?

RUPE My fault. Forgot my poppy, didn't I? She's gone to get me one.

GEORGE It's the first time you've been, isn't it, for a couple of years?

RUPE Must be, yeah. I wanted to see Grandad.

GEORGE Tell him all about it, the trip?

RUPE Yeah. Well, and he *is* getting on.

GEORGE Yes.

RUPE Not being morbid, but you never know, right?

GEORGE No, fine. I feel the same, I suppose.

RUPE Anyway, it's not just Grandad, right, is it?

GEORGE I'm not with you.

RUPE I mean none of us know when we're going to snuff it, do we? One minute you're there, then you're zapped into extinction. Could be any minute of your life, doesn't matter how old you are.

GEORGE Very philosophical, Rupe.

RUPE No, but this could be the start of my last minute, or my last hour, or my last month.

GEORGE I think you're starting to *verge* on the morbid now, at least. It's more likely the start of your last sixty years.

RUPE I suppose.

GEORGE How was it, then? How's Jen?

RUPE Great. Really happy. She loves it.

GEORGE Good.

RUPE She loves the work, yeah? Well, it's not like work, I don't think, for her. It's just her life.

GEORGE Did she manage to get some time off, show you around?

RUPE A bit, yeah. She took me up the north of the island for a couple of days. It's even more basic up there. The second city. Well, "city". I stayed on for another day, 'cause Jen had to get back to enrol the new year. Oh, she sends her love.

GEORGE Has she got herself a boyfriend yet?

RUPE Yeah. Crazy Norwegian guy. Broke his wrist when I was there. Fell off the school roof trying to fix the guttering before the rains come.

GEORGE Are they serious?

RUPE She's talking about staying on for another year. *He* is, right? She told me not tell anyone, so don't mention it to Mum, will you? The staying on, I mean, not the boyfriend.

GEORGE No. All right.

RUPE I don't think it's just him. I mean that's nice for her, but it's really because she gets off on what she's doing. The work and the life.

GEORGE "Marching to a different drummer."

RUPE Where did Mum get that from?

GEORGE *takes the book out of the bag and hands it to* RUPE.

GEORGE Funnily enough it's in here. She asked me to bring it up for her. We both had one when we were kids. I hung on to them for some reason. Mine was all where we'd been, what we'd done, what we'd had to eat on the picnic. Dull, really. But hers has got more thoughts, ideas. A commonplace book, I think they call it.

RUPE Do they? Where's this drummer thing?

GEORGE Near the back. Yes, there.

RUPE *(reading)* "If a man does not keep pace with his companions, perhaps it is because he hears a different drummer. Let him step to the music which he hears, however measured or far away."

GEORGE It's Thoreau. Heard of him?

RUPE No. *(He leafs through the book, occasionally stopping and reading.)*

GEORGE Very quotable, Thoreau. The one I remember goes... something like, "The youth gets all his materials together to build a bridge to the moon, and when he's middle-aged he ends up building a shed with them." Something like that.

RUPE Yeah?

GEORGE I don't suppose American Lit. comes into Human Resource Management much.

RUPE No.

GEORGE Not that Thoreau wasn't an extremely resourceful human. Built his own cabin, lived in the woods.

RUPE *chuckles.*

What?

RUPE Bit about you, that's all.

GEORGE What?

RUPE Gran's taken you and Mum to Portsmouth to see the *Victory. (reading)* "Honestly, my brother is the giddy limit. Mummy and me had to go looking for him and we did not find him 'til nearly teatime and we nearly missed the..." – what? "Chara"?

GEORGE Chara. Charabanc. Coach.

RUPE Right. "...and it was very 'aggeravating' and when we found him he was talking to a sailor."

GEORGE Yes.

RUPE Three exclamation marks.

GEORGE He was telling me all about the different ships.

RUPE Oh, yes?

GEORGE I was only nine or something, Rupe.

RUPE It was a joke, George.

GEORGE Yes. It *is* quite funny, I suppose. Look, I'm not sure you should be reading that.

RUPE *You* have.

GEORGE Well, yes.

RUPE She won't mind.

GEORGE She might.

RUPE She won't. Honest.

   GEORGE *shrugs.* **RUPERT** *carries on flipping through.*

GEORGE That was the first time I remember thinking about old things as having life, that visit. Connecting with the past, with people. It was the cabins on the *Victory*. Beautifully fitted out, lovely wood, and tiny little bunks. And you realized how people were so much shorter then, and it made it easier to picture them...and I don't know, it brought them all to life for me somehow.

RUPE Stefan was the same like that, wasn't he?

GEORGE Yes, he was.

RUPE This must have been when she was older. It's just before the drummer bit. "Daddy's been away in Kenya for ever, and I get really worried about him being over there. They kill British soldiers in horrible ways, the Mau Maus. Mum throws the paper away accidentally on purpose when there's something nasty about Kenya in it, but I always have a look anyhow. Daddy might die one day just like that and I don't want him to. But he might. And I don't understand why we have to ask forgiveness on Sunday for following the devices and desires of our own hearts. If *I* died, and I hadn't followed the desires of my heart, I'd be jolly well furious. I asked George why we shouldn't follow them and he said because God would be angry."

GEORGE George was wrong. George was very priggish at that age.

RUPE I saw someone die.

GEORGE What?

RUPE When I was on my own, after Jen had gone back to the school. Killed.

GEORGE God.

RUPE In the market. He'd tried to pick my pocket earlier, at least I think so, looking back. Bumped into me, it was crowded, and he was a bit feely saying sorry. And then about half an hour later all the traders were packing up for the day, and there was this blind woman, I mean not just blind, but deformed when she stood up I saw, and she'd been there all morning squatting against a wall, keeping out of the sun, and people were chucking coins down for her, and she'd got a pile of it by the end in this scarf she had, and this bloke, the one who bumped into me, walked past and bent down, and I thought he was going to give her money, but he snatched the scarf. So she grabbed his leg. And then he smashed her round the face with the scarf, all the money in it, yeah? So it was like a cosh. And then he legged it. Tried to, but there was this van and the driver saw what happened, I mean lots of people did and they started chasing him, and he got cornered and they were all shouting and the van just drove straight at him, smashed him against the wall. And I ran over to him, nobody else did, they just stood watching, and he was still alive, didn't speak, couldn't I suppose, just looked at me for a few seconds, and then he died.

GEORGE God. How terrible.

RUPE Yeah.

GEORGE When you said "adventure". On your card.

RUPE Oh, yeah. No, that was something else, afterwards. I haven't told anyone about the market, 'til you.

GEORGE Not Jen, your mother?

RUPE No. I could have told Jen, but I wanted time to... I don't know...

GEORGE Absorb it?

RUPE I suppose. And Mum would just get upset.

GEORGE Do you keep much from her?

RUPE Only things I think would get her into a state.

GEORGE I think with May, it's the small things that get her into a state. She's good with the really important things.

RUPE Yeah?

GEORGE You can trust her, Rupe, whatever...your really important things are.

RUPE Anyway, the adventure. They all started shouting at me in the market, well, probably trying to explain, trying to justify it, right? And it was so bloody hot and this smell of all the spices and it was making me feel well sick and I had to get away. So I just walked and walked, not paying much attention and then I threw up and then I found myself in the jungle. Lost, right?

GEORGE Terrifying.

RUPE Well, not "jungle" jungle. But like there were no signposts, "this way back", and I'm lost. Total. No sense of direction. So I'm standing there, going what a bunch of bloody arse this is, yeah?

GEORGE Yeah.

RUPE And then I go, sweet, I've got this. *(He takes the compass pen from his pocket.)* I mean I've got a mental picture of the island, it's no big deal as long as I know north, south, east and west. And I've got this.

GEORGE *Very* sweet. I think that's wonderful.

RUPE The thing was bust, wasn't it? Totally wankered. I just had to guess my way back.

GEORGE Oh.

RUPE I'm going to get it repaired though, right?

GEORGE Right. *(He looks along the path.)* Here comes the poppy police.

MAY *enters. She goes straight to* RUPE *and pins his poppy on.*

MAY Hello, dear.

GEORGE How's things?

MAY *(to* RUPE*)* Stand still for goodness' sake. *(to* GEORGE*)* Oh, fine.

RUPE I can do it. You'll have the pin in me in a minute.

MAY Blast! *(She withdraws her hand and sucks her thumb.)*

RUPE Or in yourself.

MAY I put one out for him before we left home. I don't know how you missed it.

RUPE I didn't. I mean I saw it, right? I just forgot to put it on.

MAY All the way over there to get one.

RUPE I'd have gone. I said. But you said no.

GEORGE Rupe was telling me what a good time he'd had.

MAY Did he send you a card?

GEORGE Of course he did.

RUPE You know I did. I had the postcard interrogation between arrivals and the car park. Don't you remember ticking George off on your list?

MAY You! *(to* GEORGE*)* I don't have a list.

RUPE Good as.

MAY People like getting cards. Did he tell you about Jen?

GEORGE What about her?

MAY Romance.

GEORGE The boyfriend? Yes. Norwegian.

MAY Lars. Who was Lars Porsena? I was trying to think.

RUPE Who?

GEORGE Rings a bell. Poem, is it?

MAY Something. No, gone. *(She notices the walking stick.)* Is that Dad's?

GEORGE Yes.

MAY What's it doing here?

RUPE I'll take it over for him if you like.

GEORGE *(to* **MAY***)* Don't ask. *(to* **RUPE***)* Would you?

MAY There's no time now.

GEORGE I suppose not.

MAY I saw that Ginny in the ladies.

GEORGE She was here with Dad when I arrived. That's her stuff. *(He indicates the bag.)*

MAY She said. Taking a video of the parade. I told her I thought she'd be better going closer, but she said she wanted a sort of panorama of the whole thing.

GEORGE I expect she'll be down there after, zooming in tastefully on the wreaths.

MAY Dashing straight off, she said. Visiting her parents.

GEORGE Very wise of her. She's put enough backs up this morning, already.

MAY Dad?

GEORGE Among others.

MAY *looks at her watch.*

MAY She'd better get a move on.

RUPE George brought your book.

MAY *(to* **GEORGE***)* You remembered? Good. Thanks, dear. *(She picks up the book and feels it, then flips through, stopping here and there.)* Oh, yes. Things I'd forgotten. I can see myself curling up with this tonight.

RUPE Thought you were writing one of your seventy-nine-page letters to Jen.

MAY In bed, I mean. Don't exaggerate. *(to* **GEORGE***)* It'll be a good chance. Jake gets all fidgety if I read in bed.

GEORGE When's he back?

MAY Tuesday sometime. He phoned this morning.

RUPE When?

MAY I forgot to tell you. Early. Well, early for you. Not for me. You were still dead to the world.

RUPE It's Sunday.

MAY You overslept twice last week. You'll have to do better than that, Rupe, if you're going to finish your last year with good results.

RUPE If.

MAY Yes.

RUPE I mean, if I'm going to finish it.

MAY You better not let Dad hear you say things like that. What do you mean?

RUPE Nothing's certain is it? I'm just saying, if.

MAY Why wouldn't you?

A mobile phone is heard ringing from **GINNY***'s bag.*

GEORGE Bloody things.

MAY Where is she? I suppose we'd better answer it. *(She takes the phone from the bag.)* The green button, Rupe?

RUPE Yeah. Try it.

MAY *answers the phone. The clock starts to chime before striking the hour.*

MAY Hello? ...no, it's not, can I take a message for her...yes... oh...I'll tell her. Goodbye.

RUPE The red one.

   MAY *rings off.*

GEORGE What? May?

MAY Just a message for her.

RUPE She's here.

   GINNY *enters and starts to take the camcorder from the bag.*

GINNY Honestly, they bore for England, some of them, don't they? In the nicest possible way. Didn't think I'd make it.

MAY There was a call for you. A message.

   The sound of a cannon in the distance, simultaneous with the first stroke of eleven from the clock.

GINNY Thank you. What was it?

MAY Shush!

   GINNY *acknowledges her faux pas but compounds it by continuing to get the camcorder out until she becomes aware of* **MAY**'s *glare. They all observe two minutes' silence during which we hear: the approach and departure of the booming bass of a high-powered car sound system; a car alarm which screeches for fifteen seconds, stops, momentarily starts again, and then stops abruptly; and a distant shout of "wankers" in a child's voice. The cannon sounds to mark the end of the two minutes. An indistinct parade-ground order is barked. A military band starts playing a march.* **MAY** *is wiping away a tear.*

GINNY It *is* rather moving, isn't it?

GEORGE Let's see him march. He'll march better than he can walk.

GEORGE and RUPE go up the slope and look off.

MAY Who's Rory?

GINNY Was that the message? He's my cousin.

MAY What's his job?

GINNY He's a travel agent. Oh. Why?

MAY He said to tell you he's managed to get you on the earlier flight to Frankfurt this evening after all.

GEORGE Oh, God, no. May!

RUPE He's not getting up.

MAY What's happened?

MAY goes to join GEORGE as RUPE rushes back down the slope and exits along the path.

GEORGE I think he just tripped. But he's not getting up.

GEORGE and MAY follow RUPE off, leaving GINNY alone.

Scene Two

Winter. Afternoon. The bench and the litter bin have gone. Dayglo boundary tape is secured around the tree (which has been chalked with an "X") and stretches offstage. GEORGE *stands alone, looking at the tree. We hear the sound of a JCB at work which will start and stop intermittently throughout the scene.* MAY *enters.*

GEORGE Have they gone back in?

MAY It was getting a bit cold for them.

GEORGE Quite a moving little ceremony, don't you think?

MAY Very, yes.

GEORGE Seeing those old men with their caps off, heads bowed, all very conscious of time ticking away.

MAY The inscription was all right, wasn't it?

GEORGE He wouldn't have wanted anything too…over the top about himself.

MAY Pity it couldn't have gone here, in the gardens.

The JCB starts up again.

GEORGE Do you feel grown up now?

MAY Yes. Funny. Do you?

GEORGE Yes. No.

MAY Nor do I, really.

They embrace.

GEORGE Where's Rupe gone?

MAY He wanted to get something from the car.

GEORGE What?

MAY He didn't say. But he wanted us to wait here.

GEORGE He was a good dad.

MAY Yes.

GEORGE Any news on your front?

MAY The solicitors are dragging their feet. I can see it going on and on.

GEORGE I thought you'd agreed on a pretty straightforward divorce. No mucking about.

MAY I thought we'd agreed on a straightforward marriage, no mucking about. Anyway...I wish them well together.

GEORGE No, you don't.

MAY I don't wish them any harm.

GEORGE You're a good soul, know that?

MAY Not much choice. I think they run in this family, good souls.

GEORGE How's Rupe dealing with it all?

MAY Quite hurt, I think. He's trying not to let on too much.

GEORGE Have they seen each other?

MAY Once or twice. Jake's had to badger him into it though.

GEORGE I'm not surprised.

MAY I don't want Rupe not to like his father any more.

GEORGE It'll sort itself out, I'm sure.

MAY I had a big heart to heart with him last night. Rupe.

GEORGE Oh, yes?

MAY He said he thought you'd understand, and I could talk to you about it if I wanted.

GEORGE Do you?

MAY I know what you'll say. Give in.

GEORGE Give in?

MAY It's college. He doesn't want to go back next term.

GEORGE Oh.

MAY He's found this furniture-making course in the Lake
District.

GEORGE Good for him.

MAY You think so? Really?

GEORGE If that's what he wants, yes, if it's right for him.

MAY Stupid, isn't it? All those rows with Jake about Jen doing
what she wanted. And now I don't want Rupe to do it.

GEORGE What happened to "marching to a different drummer"?

MAY Well. Jake's been marching away all right, hasn't he? *I* never
did. Never take my own advice, that's my trouble.

GEORGE Would he get a grant now?

MAY It's not that. We'd manage. I'm just being selfish, I suppose.
Empty house after all these years. He'd have started by the
time I get back from Jen.

GEORGE She is definitely doing the extra year?

MAY Yes. I think this Lars is serious. I hope I like him.

GEORGE I forgot. I meant to look it up. Lars Porsena. I'm sure
it's a poem. Can't quite get it.

MAY I just don't want an empty house.

GEORGE We'll see more of each other.

MAY Yes. Good.

The JCB sounds a little nearer. GEORGE *and* MAY *register
it.*

GEORGE We shouldn't really be here, you know.

MAY Rupe'll be back in a minute.

GEORGE It was an important place. I just wanted a little while.

MAY I wonder if he'll think to bring a brolly from the car. It's clouding over.

GEORGE It'll hold off.

MAY You seem very sure of yourself.

GEORGE I'm never that.

MAY Except when you're saying "never that".

RUPE enters with his cassette player, which he puts on the ground in order to operate it. We hear the fast-forwarded sound of speech from a loaded cassette stopping and starting as he tries to find a particular place.

You took your time.

RUPE I had to make a phone call. Dad.

MAY Oh. Was that in the car?

RUPE In the back. I didn't want you to see it.

MAY Why not?

RUPE Hang on. That's about it. *(He lets the tape play normally for a couple of seconds, so we can identify the voice as* **HARRY***'s, and then stops it.)*

MAY That's Grandad.

RUPE Yeah.

GEORGE When you came up last year that time?

RUPE Right. Remember?

GEORGE Very well, yes.

RUPE He just said some stuff. Seemed like the right place for you to hear it. Both of you. Right time, yeah?

In the distance, a sound which could be drums almost immediately becomes recognizable as thunder. The sky darkens. **HARRY** *appears from behind the tree, adjusting his flies. He is wearing his ceremonial scarlet with a*

*tricorn hat. He carries a halberd. He can be neither seen
nor heard by the other three.*

HARRY Funny. I still feel I need to go, but nothing comes out.

MAY I don't know about the right time, Rupe.

GEORGE It's still some way off.

HARRY It's not. It'll be sheeting down in a minute.

RUPE *operates the cassette player, but there's silence.*

RUPE Sorry. Pressed rewind.

MAY I don't know, George.

HARRY *I* do.

RUPERT *starts to re-cue the tape again, making the
occasional mistake, until he finds the right place.*

GEORGE No, it'll hold off long enough.

HARRY Like talking to a brick wall. You'll get soaked. Come to
think of it, it's more like you're in a coma, see, George? And
you, May, and Rupert. I keep on at you because something
will get through. Now and then. Or it might, anyway. I
reckon it happened just now, down by my new bench. They
were all having a read of the inscription and I bent down
next to Clarkie. "Go on, you miserable old bugger, shed a
tear for me." And when I looked, he was. I think so, anyway.
The state his eyes are in, it's hard to be sure.

RUPE *finds the right place.*

RUPE This is it.

HARRY Do you have to, Rupert? You'll embarrass me.

The tape starts to play.

(tape) ...and I was just talking to your uncle George about
lasting, about what happens when we fall off the twig, how
we live on. If we do. And I said to him it was all about

trees and fertilizer...and now you ask me, it's not, I don't think. Not just. The trees *are* important, and so are the things people have made. We live in them, we read them, we hear them. And we have to look after them. But mostly it's people, don't you think, Rupert?

RUPE *(tape)* Yeah. I suppose.

HARRY *(tape)* I'm so glad you remembered the names of the trees, boy.

RUPE *stops the tape.*

Not bad, Harry. Quite a good stab at it, though I say so myself.

RUPE There's a bit later on as well... *(He starts to wind on the tape.)*

HARRY Go on, if you must. About how much I love you all I suppose.

RUPE ...It's just about how fond of you he was.

HARRY Loved. Love.

MAY *looks up at the darkening sky.*

MAY It was a nice idea, Rupe. Thank you. But can we go somewhere else?

HARRY I'm sure I said "loved".

GEORGE *(to* **RUPE***)* It's not long, is it?

RUPE Couple of minutes.

MAY I don't want to get soaked.

HARRY She's right, Rupert.

RUPE Right. *(He stops the tape.)*

HARRY *(to* **MAY***)* Don't you want to know about the phone call?

MAY How was Dad?

RUPE Fine.

HARRY Tell her. Go on.

MAY And?

RUPE And what?

MAY It's obviously something important.

HARRY Yes.

RUPE This course.

MAY Oh.

RUPE I told him about it.

MAY I warned you. You know your father.

RUPE Yeah. But the thing is, he said yes. He said I should do it, right? And he said he'd cough up the fees and everything.

HARRY *(to MAY)* Your face.

MAY He said what?

RUPE Yeah, I know. *(to GEORGE)* It's called cabinet making but there's design *and* restoration.

GEORGE So if you build a chair that falls apart when a real person sits on it, you'd be able to put it together again.

RUPE Something like that.

MAY Wonderful, isn't it, George? All those years... I mean, do you know the two most damning things Jake can say about someone? "Do-gooder" and "arty-farty". And now...just because he's changed his life...changed mine, it's suddenly all right. It's all right to follow the desires of your own heart. It's got the stamp of approval. From a man who once told me he'd married me because I wasn't "silly". "Silly?" I said. "Yes, dear, you've got your feet on the ground, not your head in the clouds." Well, I like clouds sometimes. Or I did.

RUPE Yeah. Well, life's a bitch.

MAY That's a horrible expression. I wish you wouldn't use it.

RUPE I got it off George.

GEORGE Thanks.

RUPE *(to* **MAY***)* Well?

HARRY He only wants to build a bridge to the moon, May. Let him try.

MAY Don't just come home when you want your washing done.

RUPE No. Right. *(He takes the cassette from the player.)* I was thinking, I could do a copy of this, to take out to Jen when you go.

HARRY Give her my love.

MAY She'd like that, yes.

RUPE Thanks.

> **MAY** *hugs* **RUPE**.

You're squashing.

GEORGE Got it.

RUPE What?

GEORGE *(to* **MAY***)* Lars Porsena. Mum made you learn it. To recite to Dad. "Lars Porsena of Clusium / By the Nine Gods he swore..."

MAY Yes. Of course. Horatio defending the bridge. "And how can man die better / Than facing fearful odds..." Dee dum dee dum dee dum dee dum...

> **MAY** *mouths along with* **HARRY** *as he repeats the lines.*

HARRY "And how can man die better / Than facing fearful odds..."

> **MAY** *stops, still unable to remember.*

"For the ashes of his father / And the temples of his Gods?"

MAY Oh, yes.

GEORGE Well remembered.

HARRY Don't mention it.

MAY Come on, then. I'm starving. And freezing. Let's have a curry somewhere.

RUPE Right.

> **MAY** *and* **RUPE** *start to move off.* **GEORGE** *hovers.*

HARRY Sharpish then, or you'll all get soaked.

GEORGE No, we won't.

MAY Won't what? Come on, dear.

> **MAY** *and* **RUPE** *exit.*

HARRY Don't contradict your old man.

> **GEORGE** *turns and looks around as if he might just have heard* **HARRY**, *then looks up, puts out his hand and feels the first drop of a sudden violent downpour. He exits. Thunder overhead becomes the beating of a drum. The JCB starts, much closer than before.* **HARRY** *moves to the tree with his halberd, and braces himself, defensively.*

PROPERTY LIST

Newspaper (**HARRY**)	p.1
Football	p.1
Umbrella (**GEORGE**)	p.1
Mobile phone (**HARRY**)	p.7
Umbrella case (**GEORGE**)	p.9
Muddy shoes (**GEORGE**)	p.12
Cassette recorder (**RUPE**)	p.12
Walkman, headphones and shirt (**RUPE**)	p.14
Clothes-shop carrier bags (**MAY**)	p.14
Top and swimsuit	p.15
Fiver (**HARRY**)	p.21
Large, radio-controlled model JCB	p.24
Envelope (**GEORGE**)	p.27
Two ice lollies and a can of coke (**HARRY**)	p.31
Tissue in a handbag (**MAY**)	p.33
Fountain pen (**GEORGE**)	p.35
Gardening gloves (**MAY**)	p.38
Briefcase with mirror, two glasses and half a bottle of champagne (**GINNY**)	p.39
Model JCB	p.41
Remembrance poppies	p.42
Camera bag with camcorder (**GINNY**)	p.42
Small carrier bag with book inside (**GEORGE**)	p.48
Walking stick (**HARRY**)	p.52
Compass and pen (**RUPE**)	p.62
Poppy (**MAY**)	p.62
Mobile phone in **GINNY**'s bag	p.65
Cassette recorder (**RUPE**)	p.71

SOUND EFFECTS

Sound of an approaching helicopter	p.5
Helicopter is now overhead	p.6
Noise diminishes	p.6
A clock chimes the quarter hour in the distance	p.7
A mobile phone rings	p.7
Distant clock chimes before striking twelve	p.18
Clock chimes the quarter hour	p.31
Sound of an approaching helicopter	p.42
Helicopter is now overhead	p.42
Noise diminishes	p.42
Clock chimes the half hour	p.44
Clock chimes the three-quarter hour	p.56
Mobile phone rings	p.65
Clock starts to chime before striking the hour	p.65

The approach and departure of the booming bass of a high-powered car sound system; a car alarm which screeches for fifteen seconds, stops, momentarily starts again, and then stops abruptly; and a distant shout of "wankers" in a child's voice. The cannon sounds to mark the end of the two minutes. An indistinct parade-ground order is barked.

A military band starts playing a march	p.66
Sound of a JCB at work, starts and stops through scene	p.68
Fast-forwarded sound of a speech, starting/stopping	p.71
Tape plays normally for a couple of seconds	p.71
Thunder in distance	p.71
RUPE re-cues the tape	p.72
Tape recording of **HARRY** starts to play	p.72
RUPE stops the tape	p.73
Thunder and rain	p.76
JCB starts much closer	p.76

VISIT THE SAMUEL FRENCH BOOKSHOP AT THE ROYAL COURT THEATRE

Browse plays and theatre books, get expert advice and enjoy a coffee

Samuel French Bookshop
Royal Court Theatre
Sloane Square
London
SW1W 8AS
020 7565 5024

Shop from thousands of titles on our website

 samuelfrench.co.uk

 samuelfrenchltd

 samuel french uk

Lightning Source UK Ltd.
Milton Keynes UK
UKHW021956170419
341193UK00005B/163/P